SINATRA

OL' BLUE EYES REMEMBERED

BY DAVID HANNA

BELL

Contents

WHAT

"**F**rank has the widest range of talent out here. With him, there's always excitement. You feel it the moment he gets on stage, So do the other performers He's a performer's performer."
—JERRY WALD, producer

"**H**e seems to enjoy carrying on his feuds even when, as with me, the other party doesn't know how it came into being or why it continues."
—LOUELLA PARSONS, columnist

"**I** remember that we were doing a two-shot scene in **Take Me Out to the Ball Game**. They set the cameras to take a close-up of Frank. 'Hey,' he said, 'what about my little girl?' So, they rearranged the set-up and gave the close-up to me."
—BETTY GARRETT, actress

"**I** always knew he'd end up in bed with a boy."
—AVA GARDNER, on hearing of the Sinatra-Farrow marriage

"**I** consider Frank the most superb entertainer of this age. When he's in good voice and a good mood, he's ahead of his field, and no one can equal him."
— HEDDA HOPPER, columnist

"**T**he only man I'd be afraid to fight is Frank Sinatra. I might knock him down, but he'd keep getting up until one of us was dead."
—ROBERT MITCHUM, actor

THEY SAY

What Sinatra has is beyond talent. It's some sort of magnetism that goes in higher revolutions than that of anybody else, anybody in the whole of show business".
—BILLY WILDER, director

Frank is very good to widows, but I wasn't interested. I didn't need the rush. I managed to say no nicely. The next day, he sent me roses."
—JOAN HARVEY, widow of producer Harry Cohn and actor Laurence Harvey

You want to take care of him. I regard Frank as my extra child.",
—JUDY GARLAND, actress

When Sinatra walks into a room, tension walks in beside him. You don't always know why, but if he's tense, he spreads it."
—STANLEY KRAMER, producer

He's the most fascinating man in the world, but don't stick your hand in the cage."
—TOMMY DORSEY, bandleader

He's kind of a Don Quixote, tilting at windmills, fighting people who don't want to fight."
—HUMPHREY BOGART, actor

Frank doesn't know how to express affection. He does it with expensive gifts."
—PHIL SILVERS, actor

Being around Frank is like living with a bear. He takes three hours to wake up in the morning. When I'm ready to go to sleep, he's up and around, full of energy and talking his head off."
— PETER LAWFORD, actor

What can I say about Frank Sinatra? Well, there's Frank Sinatra and then there are other men."
—ANGIE DICKINSON, actress

Being an 18-karat manic-depressive and having lived a life of violent emotional contradictions, I have an overactive capacity for sadness as well as elation."
—FRANK SINATRA

THE KID FROM HOBOKEN

Young Frank in
Hoboken,
circa 1919.

In 1915, as today, Hoboken, New Jersey, was a waterfront town situated just across the Hudson River from New York City, connected to it by the Hoboken Ferry. It was a busy city, thanks to its manufacturing plants, the waterfront and Hoboken's position as the hub of several railroads. In the absence of strong unions, the ethnic groups, Jews, Italians, Poles and Blacks formed tight communities and managed their own economies.

Frank Sinatra's parents, Natalie and Martin Sinatra, lived on Monroe Street in the heart of the Italian district, where Frank was born, December 12, 1915. He was baptized Albert Francis Sinatra.

Life at the very beginning was no different for Frank than for all the other Italian kids in the neighborhood. His father held down a variety of jobs until Natalie, known as Dolly, used her political connections to get him appointed to the Hoboken Fire Department. Dolly was the go-getter, working at everything from barmaid to candy maker, to supplement her earnings as a practical nurse.

Although he couldn't read music, he was soon singing with local bands.

Frank at the beginning of his career.

Young Frank spent much of his babyhood in the care of sitters and his grandmother. Dolly adored her first and only child, but the pressures of earning a living were very real. By the time Frank was ready for school, he knew his way around and could almost take care of himself. Kids grew up fast in Hoboken.

Like the other kids, he was quick with his fists and again, like other kids, got into odds and ends of mischief as he wandered around the waterfront. But unlike his pals, Frank was hung up on the new fangled gadget that had become a part of virtually every American home—the radio. He spent hours with earphones clamped over his head listening to the early radio stars, the Happiness Boys and later to vocalists Rudy Vallee, Bing Crosby and Russ Colombo. At parties, Frank liked to put on a raccoon coat, and grabbing a megaphone, croon like Rudy Vallee. When his uncle gave him a ukelele, he began to strum and sing at the political rallies Dolly was involved in. At Demarest High School he organized the glee club and was a member of the school band. A secondary interest was boxing.

After leaving school, Frank worked briefly as a copy boy on the old *Jersey Observer*. Although Frank could not read music, he soon began to appear with local bands. A radio appearance on Major Bowes' Amateur Hour led to a vaudeville tour. Homesick after three months, he returned to New Jersey where for more than a year, he worked as a singing waiter and floor show M.C. at the Rustic Cabin in Alpine, New Jersey, for $15 a week. His pay was later raised to $25, and paid his ferry fare to and from New York where he sang on radio for free.

Harry James heard him and signed Frank for $75 a week.

Frank married Nancy Barbato on February 4, 1939. The bridegroom's mother had more to do with the details of the ceremony and reception than the bride's, and to their friends, it was plain that the idea for marriage had been more Dolly's than Frank's. After they were married, Frank continued singing at the Rustic Cabin, while Nancy did odd jobs to prop up their income.

Nancy got her first taste of being a band wife when she toured with Frank during his Harry James period. It ended abruptly

Growing up, Frank was like any of the kids raised in his tight, ethnic community— except for a burning desire to be the greatest singer who ever lived.

swooned whenever Frankie, as he was quick to be called, appeared on the stages of the nation's swankiest houses.

The Paramount in New York, once the flagship of Rudy Vallee and Bing Crosby, became his. Still, Frank's meteoric rise to the top wasn't all based on talent. Frank enjoyed the help of press agent George Evans, who latched on to the singer at the Paramount stage of his career. He created the stunts, built the Sinatra fan clubs, and served as front man whenever Frank's fiery temper led him into his infamous altercations.

Sinatra was hired for the top-rated radio show, *Hit Parade*, but

By 1942, Frank Sinatra was accepted as the best band singer in the business, and no one was more aware of this than Frank.

after the band went broke in Los Angeles because James was involved in a court case and the club they were scheduled to work, the Palomar, burned to the ground.

Frank broke his contract with James to join Tommy Dorsey. Dorsey realized Sinatra's talent was special, and pushed him into the position of a featured act with the Dorsey band. Band singers of the era weren't often treated with the respect Dorsey offered Sinatra, and the two were a winning combination. The public was quick to respond to the Sinatra talent, and the smouldering sex appeal the skinny singer exuded.

In his Sinatra biography, Don Dwiggens wrote: "The Dorsey influence on Sinatra has been likened to DuMaurier's creation of Trilby from an unknown Parisian laundress, at the hands of Svengali. Frank's voice began to take on the same qualities that made Jack Leonard a top vocalist. Leonard's walking out on Dorsey had opened the door for Sinatra."

Sinatra was a hard worker, a good pupil and a talented singer to begin with. Dorsey directed that talent, developing his sense of timing with metronome precision.

By 1942, Frank Sinatra was accepted as the best band singer in the business and no one was more aware of this than Frank. He knew he would have to split with Dorsey and go out on his own as a solo star. He also knew it would be a challenging and frightening world out there. But it had to be done; he now had his first child, Nancy, to take care of, as well as his wife.

He made the break and the rest is history. Frank Sinatra became the idol of the 40's. The phrase bobby soxer came into the language then to describe his fans, the kids who screamed, yelled and

In Hollywood, the Sinatras began the kind of life poor kids from Hoboken could only dream about. On this page, Nancy, Frank, Jr. and Nancy, Jr. enjoy the front lawn and the swimming pool. At the studio, Frank attends to career business. Eventually, Sinatra would build a ranch house in Palm Springs, which became headquarters for the vast array of Sinatra business and professional enterprises.

Frank joined Harry James' band in 1939. In 1979, they re-team to celebrate.

Frank, right, one of the Hoboken Four, on radio's "Amateur Hour," 1935. Host Maj. Bowes is center.

Marty Sinatra, Hoboken Fire Chief, tries his hat on his son, 1947.

Dolly Sinatra greets son Frank in New York on return from Rome, 1953.

Mr. and Mrs. Frank Sinatra attend the Academy Awards in 1946.

When Sinatra arrived by train in Pasadena, 1943, cops were called out to stem the "mass hysteria" generated by his teenage girl fans — all rehearsed to weep, scream and "swoon" when their idol appeared.

Frank's movie career received a jolt when he teamed with Gene Kelly in MGM's *Anchors Aweigh*, 1945.

Frank moved his family to Hollywood and began building his compound in Palm Springs.

had actually outgrown it before he even started. Hollywood became the inevitable next step. He played himself in *Reveille With Beverly*, a Columbia musical. He scored a modest success and then made a couple of films at RKO. These showed Frank skinny, but likeable, doing better by the songs than the acting. It was at MGM, where he was put under contract, that Frank came into his own as a film personality, with *Anchors Aweigh* and *On The Town*. In demand for personal appearances, motion pictures and recording, he was the phenomenon that he always knew he would be. Between 1941 and 1946, he reportedly earned $11,000,000.

Recognizing that Hollywood was the hub of the entertainment business, Frank moved his family there during this era and began the construction of his compound in Palm Springs. His confidence was enormous. George Evans continued to help build the Sinatra legend until 1949, when he died. By then, Frank had begun to surround himself with his special crew of aides, who served as bodyguards and beards for his escapades, as well as sounding boards for his hopes, dreams and frustrations. In a sense, they were his whipping boys. A few would disappear over the years, but to a man, they all knew that Frank was marked for a spectacular career.☆

A youthful Frank Sinatra steps into the studio photographer's domain for a typical Hollywood "glamour" shot.

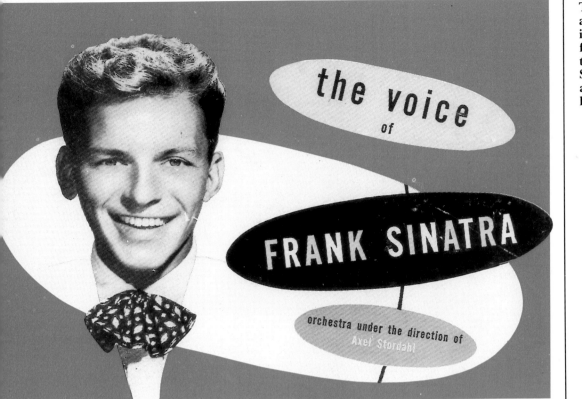

A MAN AND HIS MUSIC

Undeniably, natural talent was Frank's greatest gift. But without practice, discipline — and most importantly, a vision — that talent would not have amounted to a hill of beans.

You could feel the excitement coming out of the crowds when that kid stood up to sing. He was a skinny kid with big ears, and yet what he did to women was something awful."

Back in the days when Frank Sinatra was singing for free on New York's radio stations, among his fans was an elderly Italian singing teacher, whose pupils had appeared in opera houses the world over. With every note — even the occasional flat ones — she nodded her head approvingly. "He's great — that young man," she said. "He's like Caruso and the great Richard Tauber. Don't laugh. He breathes through his skin."

Frank Sinatra ended a short retirement with a TV special, an hour show, starring only himself.

15

In an article published in *Life* magazine on the occasion of his fiftieth birthday, Frank wrote: "It was my idea to make my voice work in the same way as a trombone or violin—not sounding like them but 'playing' the voice like those instruments. The first thing I needed was extraordinary breath control, which I didn't have. I began swimming in public pools every chance I got—taking laps under water and thinking song lyrics to myself. I worked out on the track at the Stephens Institute in Hoboken, running one lap, trotting the next one. Pretty soon, I had good breath control."

With practice, Frank—instead of singing two bars at a time—was singing six, sometimes eight bars without taking a visible or audible breath. This gave the melody a flowing, unbroken line.

He also learned to use the microphone. "Many singers never learned to use one," Frank wrote. "They never understood that a microphone is their instrument. Instead of playing a saxophone, they're playing a microphone."

Frank became a star within a few months of starting with Tommy Dorsey, when he recorded *I'll Never Smile Again*. Dorsey couldn't believe what he was seeing when he noticed how moved women were by Frank's singing. "I used to stand there on the bandstand amazed I'd almost forgot to take my solos," he said. "You could feel the excitement coming out of the crowds when that kid stood up to sing. Remember, he was no matinee idol. He was a skinny kid with big ears. And yet what he did to women was something awful."

Press Agent George Evans was responsible for capitalizing on Frank's appeal to women, especially teenagers. He was responsible not only for organizing fan clubs, but teaching them the "appropriate" way to attend a Sinatra performance. He drilled them in screaming "Frankeeee," and in the proper technique for swooning. It was all mapped out, but it would have meant nothing had Frank not delivered the goods.

John Rockwell, in his biography of Sinatra, noted the disturbance caused by the young people who assembled, thousands strong, in Times Square during those fabled engagements at the Paramount. "Pundits leapt to the attack, most of them—as they were to do again with Elvis and the Beatles—attributed precious little to Sinatra's music or his ability, through talent and originality, to thrill an audience. Instead, theories were offered ranging from Sinatra's filling a void left by absent soldiers, to mass frenzies, to the primordial mother instinct."

The fact is that Frank was changing the face of popular music. He placed emphasis on lyrics, reading meaning into them, and his taste was impeccable. Songwriters knew that songs introduced by Sinatra stood the greatest chance of becoming hits. Standards also benefited. Frank was able to turn out a hit record even when singing something like "Night and Day," which had been recorded too many times to be counted.

Henry Pleasants, the distinguished interpreter of music's impact on the American psyche, saw Sinatra this way: "The absence of any impression of art was imperative to his style. He was not presenting himself as an artist. He was presenting himself as a person, as Frankie, the skinny hollow-cheeked kid from Hoboken, with a lot of hopes, a lot of problems...and a lot of frustrations, disappointments and hang-ups. More than most singers, he has lived the life he sang about."

The wily teacher had figured out the phase in Frank's musical development that set him apart throughout his career—his extraordinary control. This control wasn't an accident. Sinatra may have been born with a natural talent for singing, but it would have been meaningless without the skill to make the voice work.

From time to time, Frank did study with teachers, especially in the era when his voice failed completely. He is generous in crediting them, but actually, Frank's first teacher was himself.

Bing Crosby was one of the singers Frank admired when he was a Hoboken teenager. They appeared together in *High Society*, 1956, but the best songs went to Bing.

Fans swarm around Sinatra and Phil Silvers, in uniform for a USO tour in 1945. Silvers claimed their long friendship ended at this time.

Dorsey couldn't believe how moved women were by Frank's singing.

It was my idea to make my voice work i the same wa as a trombor or violin—n sounding lik them, but 'playing' the voice like those instruments.

George Bishop, another Sinatra admirer, wrote: "Frank Sinatra, at his best or even at his second best, makes us feel good. Through his songs he releases us from a humdrum existence and lets us know that anything is possible. Once he gets up there in the flight of his fancy, we're carried away, and when it's all over, we're grateful to him for believing in himself because that lets us believe in ourselves."

Thirty years after the fact, in 1974, former bobby soxer Martha Weinman Lear told the *New York Times* what it was like in the '40s. " 'Frankie,' we used to scream. And that glorious shouldered spaghetti strand down there in the spotlight would croon on serenely, giving us a quick little flick of a smile or, as a special bonus, a sidelong tremor of his lower lip. Frankie was sexy. It was exciting. It was terrific."

And from Jo Stafford, "Frank could never sing a song badly."

It was this quest for perfection that put Sinatra at the top of the heap. Further down come the others, Tony Bennett, Vic Damone, Eddie Fisher, the rest. What Al Jolson was to the early years of the twentieth century, Sinatra was to the rest of it—the world's greatest entertainer. ☆

THE UNDERWORLD CONNECTION

Over the years, rumors persistently linked Sinatra to crime bosses.

In January, 1947, Hollywood—and for that matter, the United States Government—was shaken by a column written by a relative newcomer to journalism, the late Robert Ruark. Frank Sinatra, it seems, had flown from Mexico City to Havana, Cuba, and was seen in the company of Charles "Lucky" Luciano, the Mafia *capo*, who had been deported to Italy a year or so earlier.

Lucky had come to Cuba, hoping to plead his case for re-entry into the United States from a closer location than Naples, where he had chosen to live and to confer with fellow mafiosi.

Wrote Ruark: "If Mr. Sinatra wants to mob up with the likes of Lucky Luciano, the chastened panderer and permanent deportee from the United States, that seems to be a matter for Mr. Sinatra to thrash out with the millions of kids who live by his every beat... This curious desire to cavort among the scum is possibly permissable among citizens who are not peddling sermons to the nation's youth... But Mr. Sinatra seems to be setting a most peculiar example for his hordes of pimply, shrieking slaves."

The effect of the column was astonishing. The United States immediately cut off all shipments of narcotic medical drugs to Cuba, a boycott which lasted until Luciano left the island. Cuban authorities then arrested Luciano and shipped him back to Naples.

Sinatra's statement was simple: "Any report that I fraternized with

Frank was fingerprinted in Los Angeles in 1947, as he applied for a gun permit. Frequently out late at night, he said he needed the gun for protection.

goons and racketeers is a vicious lie. I was brought up to shake a man's hand when I am introduced to him without first investigating his past."

Ruark's column was the first substantive confirmation of what had long been rumored, mostly in blind column items, that Frank's career, especially in its early days, had been shaped by friends highly placed in the mob hierarchy. Just as the U.S. Government had responded quickly, so too did MGM, where Sinatra was under contract, as well as George Evans. They begged Ruark to lay off, and after one more column, which took note of the incongruity of the sudden announcement that Frank would play a Catholic priest in his next picture, *The Miracle of the Bells*, and his $100,000 salary would be donated to the church, the newspaperman did exactly that.

The story was never laid to rest, however, and surfaced again and again over the years, whenever Sinatra was involved in a controversy, an altercation and, most particularly, when his political activities were concerned.

Luciano's Cuban caper was a major event in mob operations of the time, and the Justice Department, which had Luciano under surveillance, was far from pleased that Ruark had uncovered it. The meeting, attended by a virtual who's who of the underworld—Carlo Gambino, Willie Moretti, Frank Costello et al—was intended to deal with the proliferating drug market bonanza.

Furor followed publication of a photo showing gang boss Carlo Gambino (circled) among well-wishers in Frank's dressing room in 1976. The U.S. Attorney's office obscured man in bottom left.

Frank rehearses for a TV appearance with Christine, Phyllis and Dorothy, the McGuire Sisters, in 1957.

It took 36 suites at the Hotel Nacional to accommodate the American gangsters—and Frank Sinatra. Sinatra had been accompanied on the trip by the Fischetti brothers, Rocco and Joseph, Florida kingpins in the Mafia hierarchy. It was reported that everyone brought envelopes of cash for Lucky, and that Frank had carried a suitcase containing two million dollars in cash.

Some years later, in a capricious moment, Sinatra pointed out the mathematical impossibility of cramming that much money into the attache case he was supposed to have toted. It got a laugh, of course, but did not really do anything to erase the suspicion that it had actually happened.

In 1968, during the height of the Presidential campaign, in which Sinatra was the fervent supporter

S aid Sinatra, "Any report that I fraternized with goons and racketeers is a vicious lie."

Phyllis McGuire and Sam Giancana, reputed Chicago crime syndicate leader, in London, 1962. Giancana was gunned down in 1975.

Frank Sinatra, arriving at the State Investigation Committee with his attorney, Bruce Kaufman, 1970. Sinatra was questioned about organized crime. The appearance followed protracted legal battles between his home state and the singer. He threatened never to perform in New Jersey again.

HOODS & HOLLYWOOD—
Familiar Bedfellows

Frank Sinatra was not the first entertainer involved with crime figures on either a personal or professional level. Wherever there is an element of show business, there is a need for money. Over the years, crime lords have been generous benefactors of the performing arts, particularly night clubs, the arena of saloon singers where Sinatra was a special star. During Prohibition, the clubs of major cities were largely financed by gangsters, and after 1933, the clubs were incorporated as legitimate business. Harry Richman, Sophie Tucker, Jimmy Durante, all pioneers in gangster-dominated Las Vegas, knew their underworld proprietors from other years, other places. Gypsy Rose Lee, a dear friend of beer baron Waxey Gordon, owed a teeth straightening operation to his generosity. Gypsy led a parade of Broadway stars to Philadelphia every year in the charity shindig sponsored by South Philly's crime king, Boo Boo Huff. Thelma Todd, the beautiful blonde comedienne, who spoofed with the Marx Brothers, died mysteriously after a year or so of operating a Santa Monica restaurant for the mob. Phyllis McGuire was the sweetheart of Sam Giancana. Florenz Ziegfeld put his fabled Follies together with the help of mob money. Columbia Studios was founded and run as the empire of Harry Cohn, a producer who frequently leaned on loan sharks for immediate cash, counting them as friendly investors. And they tell of the extraordinary day on the set of a wartime independent movie when Nelson Eddy was paid his weekly salary of several thousand dollars in cash. Black market, Mafia money. Straight-laced Eddy was horrified, flipped the money back and demanded a check. The hoods involved shook their heads, wondering how anyone could be that square.

Over the years, Sinatra was obliged to answer a congressional summons, five grand jury subpoenas, two IRS investigations and a Crime Commission subpoena in New Jersey.

Sinatra pointed out the mathematical impossibility of cramming that much money into the attache case he was supposed to have toted.

of the late Hubert Humphrey, reports of Sinatra's gangster friendship moved from the gossip columns and tabloids to the *Wall Street Journal*, where crime reporter Nichola Gage detailed Sinatra's association with the mob.

Gage resurrected the story that Sinatra had turned to Willie Moretti, a fabled New Jersey hood, to extricate him from his contract with the late bandleader, Tommy Dorsey. Not likely. Dorsey, fiercely possessive of his band personnel, had finally grown weary of Sinatra's ambitions to strike out on his own. He sold the singer's contract to the Music Corporation of America for $60,000 and regretted later that he had not been astute enough to grab a piece of Sinatra's future earnings. It was a straightforward business deal, taking months to execute and involving a battery of agents and lawyers.

However, Sinatra never forgave Dorsey for suggesting years after the fact that he'd been visited by a pair of hoods brandishing revolvers during the negotiations.

Yards of newspaper space have been devoted to Sinatra's questionable friends. Over the years, he was obliged to answer five grand jury subpoenas, two IRS investigations, a congressional summons and a Crime Commission subpoena in New Jersey.

He also appeared in a secret session before the Kefauver Committee in 1950 and there, as always, denied anything but a casual acquaintanceship with any of the gangsters whose names were read to him. His denials continued, even in the face of photographs showing Sinatra dining with Luciano in Havana, or in a group photo with Carlo Gambino and others. He denied being friendly with Sam Giancana, although it was virtually impossible for anyone working in Las Vegas, as Frank Sinatra has done, to avoid contact with the gregarious hood.

When Giancana showed up at the Lake Tahoe-Neva Lodge, the resort partly owned at the time by Frank, Nevada's gaming board feared his presence in the area would reflect unfavorably on the state's gaming industry. State officials began formal proceedings which would strip his casino of its gambling license. Rather than see this happen, Frank turned in his license voluntarily and sold his interest in the Lodge.

And so it went throughout his business career. Sinatra was always able to retreat successfully when the questioning became too uncomfortable. It cost him money and associations. A supporter of John Kennedy, he was quietly banished from Camelot when Attorney-General Bobby Kennedy warned the president about the Sinatra-Giancana connection. Hence Frank's support of Humphrey in '68, when the Democratic primaries pitted Humphrey against Bobby Kennedy. The latter's assassination, of course, led to Humphrey's nomination, but in the final campaign, Sinatra's work was muted.

Later, less was written about Sinatra's so called Mafia ties. Sinatra always lived by an image. We saw a number of them, the bobby soxers' idol, the serious actor, the philanthropist, etc. Later we had Sinatra, the senior citizen, eminently respectable and eager to avoid confrontations with his past.

Sinatra once explained his philosophy of dealing with questions. "There are two ways to answer a question. One is 'yes.' The other is 'no.' It's smarter, kid, to always answer 'no' until you're sure what 'yes' involves."

This, clearly, was the technique Sinatra employed to survive the numerous inquiries into his Mafia relationships. ☆

By 1949, Frank's reputation as a swinging man about town made it clear that the Sinatra marriage was doomed. For a while, it appeared that Lana Turner might become the catalyst. This changed dramatically after Frank and Ava Gardner turned a casual acquaintanceship into a dramatic, volatile affair, believed to have been ignited when they spent an evening together, drinking and doing the rounds until the small hours of the morning. The locale changes from chronicler to chronicler. It might have been Palm Springs, New York or Houston.

Frank had seen Ava in films and admired magazine cover shots of

AVA

The one great love in Sinatra's life would prove to be the most devastating.

Sinatra's romance with Ava shattered the perception that opposites attract... both smoked, drank, cursed, and lived by their own rules.

the breathtaking Southern beauty with luminous skin, languid, green eyes, Botticelli lips, and a figure that cried out for a sculptor to immortalize it.

Wherever it ignited, the spark is not the question. It happened, and from that point there seemed no turning back from an explosion that shattered the perception that opposites attract. They couldn't have been more alike. Both were iconoclasts, individualists who lived by their own rules. They smoked, drank and cursed a lot. "It takes talent to live at night," Ava often said, and she and Frank enjoyed nothing more than proving it. They thrived on partying and drinking until morning. They were bright people who spoke their minds and shared the same political beliefs.

Ava gave the impression of being insecure, Frank of being supremely confident. Actually, each had something of both qualities in their characters.

The first photographed coupling of Ava and Frank is believed to have occurred in 1950 when Frank appeared at Glenn McCarthy's Shamrock Hotel. They sneaked away to a spaghetti house where a local newsman asked to snap a picture. Frank jumped from the table, yelling, "Get away, you creep!" Ava covered her face with her hands.

They were in trouble from the start, and Frank's problems were especially serious. Personally, there was his estrangement from Nancy. Professionally, he was locked in battle with MGM about his contract. He was unhappy with Columbia Records and deplored the kind of songs he was expected to sing on *Your Hit Parade*. Ava, on the other hand, having graduated from Andy Hardy pictures to films like *One Touch of Venus* and *Show Boat*, was coming into her own as an actress. Moreover, she had survived two

short-term marriages to Mickey Rooney and Artie Shaw.

Ava was definitely hot copy, and any liaison with someone of Sinatra's stature meant that the press would hound them. From Palm Springs, they raced to Mexico; later to London and Madrid, trying to stay one step ahead of the photographers and reporters. This only heightened interest and worsened their own dispositions. At home, Nancy began talking to lawyers.

Ava and Frank, welcomed in Hawaii, a stop on the mercurial honeymoon.

Ava, like Garbo, was described as the star who made love to the camera.

AVA—Her Dreams of Frank

Over the years there were rumors of an impending reconciliation between Ava and Frank. There were reunions around the globe; Madrid, Melbourne, Rome, London, as well as long telephone conversations at any hour of the day or night Ava chose. Frank was always there. But as Ava became more European, she began to see flaws in Frank. She deplored his arrogance. She loathed the Sinatra entourage of tough guys. She disliked the Sinatra playgrounds—Hollywood, Las Vegas, New York and Florida. Petty details colored her view of Frank—the too sharp clothes, the small-brimmed straws, the bow ties. Even his hep language.

Early in 1968, Frank was suffering the trauma of divorcing Mia, filming Lady In Cement by day, and singing at Miami's Fountainbleau at night. When he collapsed and was hospitalized, Ava suddenly appeared at his bedside, disguised in a blonde wig and dark glasses. Reports have it that she was available and expected Frank to appreciate the fact. She knew, and Frank knew, that they were—or had been—each other's one great love. But Ava had changed greatly in the fifteen years since their separation. Now it was Frank who saw flaws. Ava's face plainly showed the effects of years of dissipation. Her sloppy, casual attire, consisting of shirts and slacks, turned Frank off. He was even dismayed by her language. Frank preferred to idealize the women in his life.

During Frank's recovery, Ava managed to hide away in a Miami hotel, visiting him every day. But whatever her hopes for a reconciliation, such plans were doomed. Frank would remain a special friend. Nothing more. As soon as he was well enough, Frank returned to Palm Springs; Ava, to London, where the telephone remained her link to her dreams of Frank.

First stop on their honeymoon was Miami, where photogs grabbed this lonely shot of Ava and Frank on the beach.

From the moment vows were exchanged, friends predicated a short life for the marriage.

Ava Gardner and Frank are all smiles at their wedding, November 8, 1951.

27

Ava as a blonde! It happened once or twice, and no one knew what Frank thought of it. Ava wasn't sure herself.

Sinatra followed Ava to Spain, where she was shooting *Pandora and Flying Dutchman* and being courted by bullfighter Mario Cabre. Frank showed up with a $10,000 necklace and Cabre disappeared. When Ava returned to the studio they got together in Palm Springs and Lake Tahoe.

On August 16, 1951, Frank established residence in Reno and waited out the six weeks before a divorce could be granted with a raging engagement. He was treated for an overdose of sleeping pills. After Nancy got her decree in California, Frank obtained his.

Ava's eyes were starry when the stormy courtship ended and they were married on November 7, 1951, at the Philadelphia home of the late theatrical agent, Manny Sacks. The past was forgotten, not only in the thrill of marriage, but in the frenzy to avoid press coverage.

From the moment vows were exchanged, friends predicted a breakup of the marriage. Sinatra's decline was real, financially and vocally. His voice had faded and there were those who believed he would never sing again. High taxes, high living, lavish generosity and the cost of a huge settlement with Nancy had left him with little reserve.

Ava put less priority on her own success than seeing Frank through this dark period of his career. There wasn't a doubt in her mind

that once he hit the comeback trail, he would be bigger than ever. She supported his spectacular idea of selling himself for the role of Maggio in *From Here to Eternity* and took part in the highly publicized campaign, to the extent of telephoning producer Harry Cohn and his wife, Joan.

Throughout 1952, Ava followed Frank from night club to night club, many of them spots that he would never have considered playing a year earlier. Sinatra's voice was in bad shape, a fact not unnoticed by the press. This didn't help matters, nor did Ava's incredible jealousy.

There has always been confu-

Wherever they went, whatever they did, Ava and Frank were objects of photographers' interest.

In an effort to get Ava's attention, Sinatra pumped bullets into a pillow in a phony suicide scare.

Ava, at Portofino, with Humphrey Bogart, for *The Barefoot Contessa* (1954).

sion in people's minds about who did what to whom in the Sinatra marriage. Ava's jealousy was intense, and years later, she would admit it. It was difficult for Frank to handle, particularly in light of his own professional problems.

At the Copacabana in New York one night, Ava was seated at ringside. Marilyn Maxwell, an old flame of Frank's, walked in and Frank nodded to her. Ava noisily left the club, departing for her world of nocturnal hideaways, Harlem, jazz joints, even the apartment of former hubby Artie Shaw.

At the Hampshire House, before their marriage, Sinatra had pumped bullets into a pillow in a phony suicide scare. Ava refused to open the door. David O. Selznick was on the same floor, and he helped Frank and Ava dispose of the incriminating evidence before the police arrived to inquire about the gun shots.

Their marriage was more of the same. Ava threw tantrums whenever she couldn't find Frank's whereabouts. She poured out her heart to Dolly Sinatra, who was thoroughly taken with her son's beautiful second wife, and she pleaded with directors to arrange shooting schedules of her pictures so that she could be with Frank.

By the end of 1953, when she was loaned to Joseph L. Mankiewicz for *The Barefoot Contessa*, the marriage was in a shambles. As she left for Rome to do the picture, arriving weeks before she was needed, MGM announced the Sinatras' separation.

There was a spectacular attempt at a reconciliation. At Christmas, Ava flew to Madrid and Frank, getting wind of it, raced there to be with her. Ava returned to Rome with Frank, both looking weary, tired and disgruntled. They gave a New Year's Eve party, but that was all Rome saw of them for the several days Sinatra remained. He sneaked out quietly, managing to elude the press, so no one knew if there had been a reconciliation, until Ava sadly said, "No."

Not long afterward, bullfighter Luis Miguel Dominguin arrived in Rome to keep Ava company during the filming of *Contessa*. At the studio, Ava's phonograph blared Sinatra records throughout the day. Co-star Humphrey Bogart grumbled, "That's nuts. One Sinatra is worth a dozen bullfighters."

Ava obtained a Nevada divorce in 1957. ☆

FROM HERE TO ETERNITY

As an actor, Frank discovered discipline for the first time, turning in the performance of his career in the part he was born to play.

When Mario Puzo's novel *The Godfather* was published, columnists and readers alike saw similarities between Sinatra and the fictional character, Johnny Fontaine. Fontaine was a singer catapulted into prominence by the mob. In one chapter, a movie producer, reluctant to employ Fontaine, awakens to find the severed head of his prize horse in bed next to him.

Smarting at the comparison, Frank said that he gave author Mario Puzo a piece of his mind one night when they bumped into each other at Chasen's. "What phony stuff!" he said. "Somebody going to the mob to get a movie role. Puzo's a bum. I screen tested for the role, and Harry Cohn hired me."

The role he was referring to, of course, was Maggio in *From Here to Eternity*. From the moment he'd read the book, Frank identified with the skinny, gritty Italo-American stationed at Pearl Harbor. In Maggio, Frank saw himself, and every kid in Hoboken he'd ever known.

After personally asking Harry Cohn for the part and offering to do it for $8,000, Frank enlisted his agents, Ava, the public and friends to put the pressure on the producer, one of Hollywood's legendary despots. After tests were made, including one of Sinatra, the final choices narrowed to Eli Wallach and

Sinatra came into his own as an actor in *From Here To Eternity*. He's seen with co-stars Montgomery Clift and Burt Lancaster.

Producer Harry Cohn took Frank at his word, paying $8,000 for a star whose fee was usually $150,000.

Frank. Everyone agreed that Wallach was the better actor, but there was little doubt that physically and emotionally Sinatra, as he had claimed, actually *was* Maggio.

Everything about Frank and *Eternity* was dramatic. He had flown to Nairobi to be with Ava during the filming of *Mogambo*. Five days after he arrived, he was summoned back to test, even paying his own way. Then came the waiting, and finally, the deal. Harry Cohn took Frank at his word, paying $8,000 for a star whose fee had previously been $150,000 a picture.

With the contract in his hand, Frank felt good inside for the first time in months. He was the old Sinatra, the guy who could do anything. Still, he knew there was much to learn. He would need more than his instinctive abilities as a performer, his years of singing to live audiences, and his work at MGM. One thing was clear—he was no longer Frank Sinatra, the romantic singer. He now had a new vitality; the urge to create a meaningful character. Audiences would have to understand Maggio as clearly as Frank knew him.

How lucky Sinatra was, and to his credit, he admitted it repeatedly over the years, that Montgomery Clift had been assigned to play Pruett. They became

Sinatra, Clift and Lancaster in *Eternity*.

instant buddies. Frank was awed by Clift's versatility as an actor. Even Burt Lancaster admitted to being more than just a little intimidated. But Monty was a friendly young man, eager to share his knowledge with Frank. Away from the set, they worked together for hours, perfecting the details of their characterizations.

And when it was over, they boozed and passed the time talking about life and love. They spent countless hours trying to get through on the telephone to Nairobi and Ava. And of course no Sinatra appearance—even playing Maggio—was free of Sinatra temperament. Sinatra decided to sit down for one scene, despite Fred Zinneman's insistence he play it standing up. This impasse persisted until Harry Cohn strode onto the set and ordered Sinatra to obey the director's orders.

Discipline was restored and the payoff came the

Away from the set, Sinatra and Clift worked together for hours, perfecting details of their characterizations.

following April when Frank, accompanied by li Nancy and Frank, Jr., accepted the Academy Aw for Best Supporting Actor. (Ava was a nominated—as Best Actress for *Mogambo*.) Critics a the public hailed Frank as a skilled dramatic act Sinatra had kept his word; he'd promised to come b and start over again. But not even the celebra Oscar win could foresee the huge changes his car would now embrace: film star, TV star, concert st film and record producer, businessman, philanthro and political maverick.

After the Awards ceremony, Sinatra voiced regret. "I forgot to thank Monty Clift for all the help gave me." They remained firm friends until, accord to one Clift biographer, Monty made a pass at a m guest during a party at Sinatra's home. That, sa ended the friendship.

32

The payoff came when Frank, accompanied by little Nancy and Frank, Jr., accepted the Academy Award for Best Supporting Actor.

Frank in his dressing room, preparing to face cameras as Maggio, the role he begged to play.

Sinatra has won three awards from the Academy of Motion Picture Arts and Sciences. His first, a Special, came in 1945 for *The House I Live In,* a 10-minute short that made a plea for racial tolerance. He won the Best Supporting Oscar for *From Here to Eternity* (1953) and was nominated for Best Actor for *The Man With the Golden Arm* (1955). His third Oscar was the Hersholt Humanitarian Award. In 1963 and 1968, Frank hosted the Awards ceremony.

Sinatra, holding a memento of his years of social work — the Jean Hersholt Humanitarian Oscar which was awarded to him in 1971.

Frank Sinatra
found a role close
to his own person-
ality in *Pal Joey*
(1957). Kim Nova
played opposite
him.

COMEBACK

Sinatra had to make some tough decisions.

Frank Sinatra's critical success as Maggio in *From Here to Eternity*, and the public's delight in him as a dramatic actor, energized Frank to an extraordinary degree. Within the next couple of years, he would become one of the most visible personalities on the theatrical scene, racing from film to film, and recording more enthusiastically than ever before.

Behind him were the early fifties, when he'd been jeered by fans because of the croak his voice had developed, not to mention the terror of the weeks following a Copacabana engagement, which he was forced to cancel because his voice had deserted him completely.

Whether he sang or not, Frank was still big at the box-office. In a burst of energy, he turned 1955 into a multi-million-dollar year. He appeared in a sequence of pictures that included *Young at Heart, Not as a Stranger, Guys and Dolls, The Tender Trap* and *The Man With The Golden Arm*. Capitol was pressing such best-selling Sinatra singles as *Learnin' The Blues* and *Young At Heart* and albums like *Songs For Young Lovers* and *Swing Easy*.

Sinatra made forays into television, serving as guest star on the programs of Bob Hope and others. He battled with Ed Sullivan over the MC's tradition of low pay for his artists. He was disappointed at not playing the lead in *On The Waterfront*, which

went to Marlon Brando. When he and Brando teamed in *Guys and Dolls*, evidence of Frank's displeasure with the standard techniques of rehearsals and repeated takes became evident. He told direc-

tor Joseph L. Mankiewicz to call him to the set only after rehearsing with "Mumbles" Brando. Sinatra felt that repeated takes ruined the spontaneity of his acting.

Yet, one could see that the old system had plainly benefitted Sinatra. His screen work steadily improved from picture to picture as experience — and rehearsal — brought depth to his characterizations.

For the moment, there was only success as Frank scored in picture

after picture, playing a wide variety of roles. He spoofed with Bing Crosby in *High Society*, and was a charming gigolo in *Pal Joey*. There were excellent performances in *The Manchurian Candidate*, and

some years later, in *The Detective*. Sinatra fans also enjoyed him in *Can Can*.

But for all these successes and evidence of Sinatra's increasing growth as an actor, his record began to grow

Sinatra followed *Eternity* with the melodrama *Suddenly* (1954) in which he played an assassin.

Kim Novak and Frank made an appealing romantic team in *The Man With the Golden Arm*. Film turned into a big box office hit.

For the moment, there was only success, as Frank scored big in picture after picture, playing a wide variety of roles and showing a diversity of talent.

As an addict in *The Man with the Golden Arm* (1955), Frank continued to grow as an actor. Darren McGavin shares scene.

Frank turned to comedy with Debbie Reynolds in *The Tender Trap* (1955) and scored a success.

Sinatra's skills were severely tested in the role of a World War II amputee in *Kings Go Forth* (1958), shot in Paris.

spotty. Once again Sinatra had decided his career would be molded according to his own terms. Producers knew they were getting a handful when they hired him. He withdrew from *Carousel* when he was told the picture would be made in both standard thirty-five millimeter CinemaScope and a new fifty-five millimeter screen process, requiring at least two takes for every shot. "I will not make two pictures for the price of one," Sinatra said, and he walked away from a role that was absolutely perfect for him.

In Spain, with *The Pride And The Passion*, he began demanding abbreviated shooting

Gary Cooper took time out from his own Westerns to give some tips on arms when Frank went cowboy in *Johnny Concho* (1956).

Frank directed *None But the Brave* on location in Hawaii (1965).

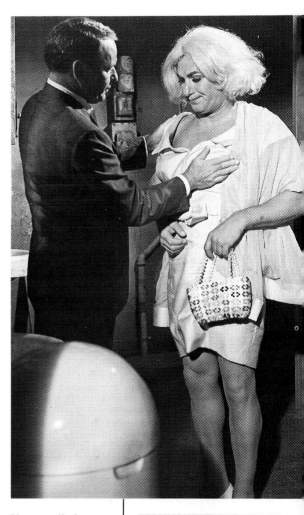

In Israel for *Cast a Giant Shadow* (1966).

schedules for himself. When filming in Hollywood, he flew in from Palm Springs, did his work and flew back every night. He began to choose his own stories and produce them as well. Then there were the Rat Pack movies, films starring his buddies: *Ocean's Eleven*, *Sergeants 3* and *Robin And His Seven Hoods*. They showed a profit, but did little to enhance Frank's career, being nothing more than fluff.

After 1970, the films dwindled to nearly

Frank checks out Pat Henry's drag in the police thriller, *Lady In Cement* (1968).

Sinatra piled up an impressive list of acting credits with action roles like that he played in *Assault On a Queen* (1966).

Dirty Dingus Magee (1970) was another Western for Frank.

Sammy Davis, Jr. and Dean Martin teamed up with Frank to make *Sergeants 3* (1961), a multimillion dollar remake of *Gunga Din.*

nothing. There was only *The First Deadly Sin* and a television movie, *Contract On Cherry Street.* In the '80s, he did an episode on *Magnum, P.I.* Sinatra, like most movie producers in decline, blamed the absence of good scripts for the decrease in the quality of his films. But the real reason lay in Frank's growing indifference to filmmaking. His private fortune was now derived from so many different projects that movie making had

become bothersome. It had accomplished its purpose—making him a superstar.

New York Times critic Bosley Crowthers mourned Sinatra's lackluster work by writing: "It is provoking—nay, disturbing and depressing beyond belief—to see this acute and awesome figure turning up time and time again in strangely tricky and trashy motion pictures." Celebrated critic Pauline Kael asked,

They began calling them the Rat Pack. Frank, Sammy and Dean co-starred in *Robin and the 7 Hoods* (1964). Frank was their leader off-screen and on.

Sinatra, Bing Crosby, Sammy Davis and Dean Martin at a 1965 recording session, held at Frank's Reprise Records.

Frank withdrew when he was told that each scene would require at least two takes. Said Frank, "I will not make two pictures for the price of one."

Dean, Sammy and Frank toured Germany in 1975. Shot was taken at Hamburg, a few minutes before Frank cancelled Berlin gig because of "nasty" German press remarks.

Dean Martin has the distinction of being Frank Sinatra's most frequent co-star. Aside from their innumerable nightclub, concert and television appearances together, they partnered in six films: *Some Came Running* (1959), *Ocean's Eleven* (1960), *Sergeants 3* (1962), *4 for Texas* (1963), *Robin and the 7 Hoods* (1964) and *Marriage on the Rocks* (1965).

The Rat Pack horned in on Sammy Davis Jr.'s act in Las Vegas, to the delight of Sammy, The Sands Hotel and the customers. Lined up are Sinatra, Dean Martin, Davis, Peter Lawford and Joey Bishop.

When Hollywood filmed the smash hit Broadway musical *Guys and Dolls* (1955), Sinatra seemed a natural to play the womanizing Sky Masterson, but producer Samuel Goldwyn cast him in the non-singing role of Nathan Detroit, while Marlon Brando, a non-singer, sang, or tried to, the role of Masterson. The results were to be expected, despite Brando's personal vocal coaching from composer Frank Loesser (above right).

Why has Sinatra not developed the professional pride in his movies that he takes in his recordings?"

Sinatra's answer was one he used frequently. When you're on a record singing, it's you and you alone. If it's bad and gets criticized, it's you who's to blame—no one else. If it's good, it's also you. But with a film, it's never like that; there are producers and scriptwriters and hundreds of men in offices and the thing is taken out of your hand." From his own point of view, Frank may have made sense. What certifies his importance for posterity is his singing, not his acting; his records, not his films.☆

Bing Crosby and Frank were paired in *High Society* (1956), the musical version of *The Philadelphia Story.*

Rare poster shows Frank teamed with the great Spencer Tracy in *The Devil at 4 O'Clock* (1961).

Another scene from *Robin and the 7 Hoods.* Frank's seen here with Hans Conreid and Bing Crosby's son, Dennis.

The question of why Sinatra accepted the job was left unanswered, unless it was to take advantage of the opportunity to make up with Ava.

"COME FLY WITH ME..."

While concerts and film appearances were legitimate reasons for hopping overseas, irrational vendettas and flights of fury were harder to justify.

In the course of his long career, Sinatra made many trips abroad. There were concerts, films and personal trips to visit friends like Princess Grace in Monaco. There were also an extraordinary number of singing appearances at charity galas. These visits did more good for Uncle Sam's foreign relations than a roomful of ambassadors and diplomats. Sinatra was proof of the universal language of music.

Then there were those other trips—punctuated by his fury and outrageous conduct. In the mid-fifties, Frank came to Spain to costar with Cary Grant and Sophia Loren in *The Pride and the Passion*, a story about Spain's war for Independence against the French. It was a costume picture, something Sinatra reportedly detested. Nor did he care for Spain. The question of why he accepted the job was left unanswered; unless it was the opportunity to make up with Ava, who at the time was making her home in Madrid. But that never happened.

His arrival was preceded by a telephone call to producer Stanley Kramer, warning that if so much as one newspaperman showed up at the airport, Frank would take the next plane back. The reasons, besides Frank's chronic aversion to the press, were immediately clear. He was carrying a trunk filled with Jack Daniels and was accompanied by a young woman, Peggy Connolly.

Yet the next morning, photos of Frank, smiling and gracious, were all over the front pages of Spain's newspapers. He had attended a ball the night before, given by the Spanish film industry. The photographs showed him smiling broadly, Peggy at his side.

Kramer was prepared for difficulties with Sinatra, but he felt that the role of a Spanish patriot who leads a ragged band of partisans across Spain pulling a huge cannon, was perfect for Frank. Kramer had braved Sinatra's stormy ways the first time he had ever gone to bat as a director. The film

...as *Not As a Stranger*, and the industry quipped that Kramer would never again have Frank in one of his films. He'd sooner go begging on the street with a tin cup, the rumor went.

During the first few weeks of *The Pride and the Passion*, Sinatra was quiet and friendly. He adored Sophia Loren, spoke to her in Italian and taught her dirty words in English. Cary Grant looked on in awe whenever Sinatra used his instinctive talents to play a scene. This was exactly the opposite of Grant's carefully rehearsed style of acting.

Midway through production, Louis Sobel, a Hearst columnist, printed a report that Sinatra had walked off the picture. Sinatra blamed the press department and wanted the head man fired. Kramer refused, knowing Sinatra had planted the item himself, a first step in his determination to

Frank and Sophia Loren in *The Pride and the Passion*. It may or may not be true that Sophia fell in love with Cary Grant during the filming in Spain. Insiders maintain it was a publicity stunt. Sophia and Frank, however, were real pals, enjoying their time together on the set.

get the shooting schedule revamped. "He's been beefing, and I'm afraid I am going to have to change the schedule."

On the home front, Peggy Connolly was in Frank's hotel suite when he got a call from Ava. "You going to see her?" Frank's new love interest asked. Frank said yes, and within hours, Peggy had left Madrid.

Frank warned Kramer that he intended leaving Spain by a certain date. In order to save his expensive project, Kramer completely revamped the schedule, and the final cut of the film showed that damage had been done. Sinatra left Madrid as threatened. There were no newsmen or members of the film company to say goodbye.

Yet when Sophia Loren was brought to America on a press tour for the picture, Kramer appreciated his cooperation in the Italian promotion, saying, "I'll never understand that man. He couldn't have been more helpful. Just great, while Grant did nothing."

In July, 1972, newspapers were filled with reports of a fracas that had occurred at Jimmy's Cafe in Monte Carlo. According to an American student, John Rhall, then 22, he was assaulted by the entertainer and a bodyguard after he took photographs of his friends at their own table in a nightclub. Rhall said Sinatra had been behaving in an excited manner, and when he saw the camera, he approached Rhall and twisted his arm, demanding to know if he was a newsman.

"Sinatra broke my Cartier watch and tore my shirt. I told him if he wanted the camera, he could have it." He said Sinatra threw the camera into the sea.

According to Rhall, at six in the morning, his hotel room suddenly filled up with a doctor, hotel security people and a bouncer from Jimmy's.

The bouncer asked, "Why do you want to cause trouble for Mr. Sinatra?"

Rhall told the intruders to get out and that he intended filing charges later in the day, which Sinatra and his pals quit Monte Carlo. Young Rhall could not afford the legal fee to press his case in a civil suit, and there the incident ended.

One of Frank's most spectacular international encounters occurred a decade earlier in Australia, a country whose press is as wild and woolly as the land down under is presumed to be. Aussie journalists had annoyed Frank at the airport and bothered him in his hotel. Of course, he had refused the usual meeting with the press which visiting celebrities are expected to endure.

The night of his first Australian concert, Sinatra paused to chat with the audience, a tendency that was to prove increasingly embarrassing for Frank, the more it became an intrinsic part of a Sinatra performance. "I'm a little tired," he said. "I had to run all day because of the parasites who chase us. It's the scandal men that bug you and drive you crazy. And the broads of the press are all hookers. I hope I don't have to explain the word 'hooker' to you. Anyhow, I'd give them about a dollar and fifty cents..."

And so it went, right into the newscasts and newspapers. The uproar was instantaneous. Sinatra was reproved in Parliament. Press unions sputtered their anger. Stagehands refused to work his show. He could not get room service in his hotel. The tour was threatened.

Finally, it looked as though union opposition to Frank would be so strong that there would be no means of transportation available to him to leave Australia unless he apologized. It didn't quite come to that, but a joint statement was issued by Sinatra and the unions that cleared the air to the point that he could quit Australia—by air.

Bob Hope quipped, "They finally let Frank out of the country, after the head of the union down there woke up with a kangaroo's head on the next pillow." ☆

When Frank arrived in Rome in 1958 for a visit with Ava Gardner, he was accompanied by the Peter Lawfords—a device to distract the press.

Sinatra adored Sophia Loren, spoke to her in Italian and taught her dirty words in English.

Kramer gave in to Sinatra's tirades and completely revamped the schedule. The final cut of the film shows the extent of the damage that was done.

Wherever he went, Frank had no trouble locating female companions. Here he's seen with Isabelle Tiberghien, a beauty queen, during a stopover in Biarritz, France, 1972.

Frank, who always enjoyed being the man about town, escorts Gloria De Haven to New York premiere of *The Sullivans* back in 1944.

When Gloria Vanderbilt ended her marriage to Leopold Stokowski in 1954, Frank was at her side in public and at home.

NOT EVERY LADY WAS A TRAMP

Sinatra spent a lifetime searching for one woman who would love him for what he was, and not try to change him.

After a scandal magazine headlined that Frank's virility came from a breakfast diet of Wheaties, sales of the cereal zoomed.

Lady Adele Beatty thought she had snared Frank after he escorted her around London in 1958. Like so many dolls in his playpen, Oklahoma-born Adele was dumped after she talked to the press about her affair with Frank.

Juliet Prowse, here with Frank in 1960, was his long-time companion until it was taken for granted they would marry. That ended the affair.

Frank Sinatra once remarked that if he'd had as many affairs as he'd been credited with, he would reside in a laboratory bottle at Harvard Medical School.

The fact is that Sinatra piled up a boudoir record that was remarkable even by Hollywood standards, where the feats of such Lotharios as Walter Pidgeon, Sonny Tufts, Forrest Tucker, Fredric March and Errol Flynn are recalled with awe.

In and out of marriage, Sinatra found time and opportunity to date starlets who have been described as anyone from a rising movie actress to "any beautiful girl not regularly employed in a brothel."

In his Sinatra biography, Don Dwiggins noted a Hollywood legend that Frank once decided to have affairs with Hollywood's top ten glamour girls, and placed their names on his studio dressing room door, checking them off one at a time in a sort of Hollywood roulette.

On the other hand, Hollywood's vice squad officers reported finding Sinatra's name popping up in the handbags of some of the handsomest Hollywood starlets. After a scandal magazine headlined that Frank's virility came from a breakfast diet of Wheaties, sales of the cereal zoomed.

Granted, Frank spent time with budding starlets, but he also dated some of the most beautiful and interesting women in the world—in show business, high society and in the political arena. To a woman, most of them remember him with great affection and one gets the impression that given the opportunity to date him again, they'd run, not walk, to whatever rendezvous point Frank selected.

Angie Dickinson, Shirley MacLaine, Carol Lynley, Marilyn Maxwell, Betty Furness, Linda Christian, Anita Ekberg, Hope Lange, Victoria Principal, Kim Novak and Judy Garland all dated Sinatra at one time or another. They maintained that among other things, he was helpful in their careers. Society figure Gloria Vanderbilt reportedly was grateful to Frank for helping her at a critical moment in her life, a time when she knew her marriage to Leopold Stokowski was over and didn't quite know how to end it.

Aside from generalities and words of praise for Frank's thoughtfulness, the women in his life were reluctant to go into detail about their affairs. Kitty Kelly, in *His Way*, her unauthorized biography of Frank Sinatra, noted: "Jealousy guarding his privacy, Sinatra built a wall of secrecy around the women in his life. He was humiliated when his affair with Shirley Van Dyke became public in 1957 after the thirty-two-year-old actress took an overdose of pills. She claimed to have known him for fourteen years.

"Frank admitted that he had obtained bit movie parts for her...but he refused to comment on her suicide note, which said: 'The one I've really loved, Frank Sinatra, you've done me wrong. You're so big and I'm so small."

For quite some time, Peggy Connolly was Frank's steady girl friend, but, like the others, she did not make it to an engagement announcement. In 1962, after they were seen together constantly, Frank and South African dancer Juliet Prowse announced they were engaged. A few months later came a

Frank's lady friends always remembered their dates with him as "special." Jill St. John, here in 1962, was no exception.

Hard to tell if Frank and Carol Lynley were being gracious to the photographer or planning to bolt his lens.

Jealousy guarding his privacy, Sinatra built a wall of secrecy around the women in his life.

Hope Lange darted in and out of Frank's little black book with refreshing regularity.

EDITH GOETZ—
Her Mouth Cost Her A Wedding Ring

Edith Goetz, according to Kitty Kelly, had a disastrous relationship with Sinatra—one of her own making. The daughter of MGM tycoon Louis B. Mayer and widow of producer William Goetz, she was appreciative of the attention Frank showed her after her husband's death. "He couldn't have been kinder." The two dated, enjoyed quiet trips together and the affair, broken off during his marriage to Mia, resumed shortly thereafter. There came a point when Frank suggested it might become permanent. Without thinking, Edie blurted out, "Why, Frank, that's impossible, you're nothing but a hoodlum." Frank picked up his hat, walked out of the house and never spoke to Edie again.

At a Hollywood premiere in the early 1950s, Frank Sinatra is seated between his date, Kim Novak, and Lauren Bacall. Bacall's husband, Humphrey Bogart, chats with Mrs. Gary Cooper.

The Rat Pack was composed of top celebrities — Bogart, Sinatra, Sammy Davis, Peter Lawford, Judy Garland, David Niven and others. According to Bogart, "We admired ourselves and didn't care for anyone else."

Vice squad officers reported finding Sinatra's name popping up in the handbags of some pretty Hollywood starlets.

Sinatra and Bacall attend the opening of Marlon Brando's *Sayonara* in 1957. A romance had developed between Frank and Betty, as Bacall was called by friends, following the death eleven months earlier of Bogey.

second announcement The engagement wa off because of career dif ferences. Inside Holly wood, it was believed the affair had been trumped up by Frank to help Juliet along in he career.

Of all the Sinatra women, sharp tongued Lauren "Betty Bacall fared mos miserably. She and Bogey had been long time friends of Frank and the Rat Pack gathered most frequent ly at their home. It wa composed of top celebrities like Bogart Sinatra, Sammy Davis Peter Lawford Jud Garland, David Nive and others. Accordin to Bogart, they existe "for the relief of boredom and th perpetuation of in dependence. We ad mire ourselves and don care for anyone else The frequently childis antics of the Rat Pack the feuds, inside disser sion, etc. were a repeatedly reported i the gossip press—to th point of overkill. Th Rat Pack eventuall died of its ow uselessness.

Betty was the de mother of th outrageous group, an in the years of Bogart illness, Frank became increasingly attentiv to the point that aft Bogey's death, Bett depended on him to a unusual degree. The dated constantly, wit Betty often serving Frank's hostess, an while she may hav dreamed of marriag she was careful abou bringing up the subjec She realized how deep Sinatra had been sca red by his failure wi Ava.

When he did pr pose, in 1958, fourtee months after Boge death, Betty admitte that she hesitated all "forty seconds." Fra left the next day f Miami—but keeping

Shirley MacLaine succeeded Lauren Bacall as unofficial den mother to the Rat Pack. She co-starred with Sinatra and Dean Martin in *Some Came Running* (1958), for which she earned a Best Actress Academy Award nomination. Though she lost to Susan Hayward for *I Want to Live*, the film was a turning point for MacLaine, who previously had been considered merely a supporting comedienne. She and Martin went on to appear in several comedies together and she and Sinatra re-teamed for *Can Can* (1960), his final musical. Ultimately MacLaine won her Oscar for *Terms of Endearment* (1983).

From the bold, new novel by the author of "From Here To Eternity"

FRANK SINATRA

DEAN MARTIN

SHIRLEY MacLAINE

M·G·M presents A SOL C. SIEGEL PRODUCTION

"SOME CAME RUNNING"

with **MARTHA HYER** · **ARTHUR KENNEDY**

NANCY GATES · LEORA DANA

Screen Play by JOHN PATRICK and ARTHUR SHEEKMAN · Based On the Novel by JAMES JONES · In CinemaScope and METROCOLOR · Directed by VINCENTE MINNELLI

secret like that was absolutely impossible. Betty confirmed the proposal to Louella Parsons, whose newspapers gave it headlines. In Miami, Frank was beseiged by reporters—and furious.

To the reporters Frank grumbled, "Marriage? What for? So I'd have to go home early?" To Ava, who telephoned after hearing the news, he said, "I was never going to marry that pushy broad."

To Betty, he said nothing after suggesting that they lay low for a while. They did not speak for six years. In her autobiography, Betty wrote: "To be rejected is hell, a hard thing to get over. But to be rejected publicly takes everything away from you. . . . He was too cowardly to tell the truth—that it was just too much for him, that he couldn't handle it."

Frank bristled at Betty's remarks, claiming there was another side to it—his. It has not yet been told, but Sinatra pals maintain that Frank's remarks to Ava summed up his feelings. He found Betty pushy.

☆

Elvis Presley chats
with Sinatra and
his daughter
Nancy at her 1969
Las Vegas night
club debut.

THE SMALL SCREEN

Spectacular on record, rivetting in concert, Sinatra was never at ease when it came to television.

Frank was showman enough to welcome Elvis home from the Army in 1960. For both entertainers, the teaming was a shrewd business move.

For his television shows, Frank recruited as guest stars pals like Bing Crosby and Dean Martin.

When entertainers like Elvis Presley introduced the beat of a new musical generation—rock 'n' roll—Frank Sinatra was quick to denounce the music as an "ugly, vicious, degenerate form of expression." He felt that Elvis appealed to music's lowest common denominator and disliked his glittery suits and blue suede shoes.

The fact that Elvis had been at the top of the charts virtually from his first national TV shows and concert appearances may have had something to do with Sinatra's opinion. Upstarts like Presley threatened Frank's own domination of American music. Sinatra and the other entertainers of his era had every reason to feel their positions were vulnerable, in view of the skyrocketing figures newcomers spelled out on the Top 10 chart. Even his death failed to dethrone Elvis. He remained The King. Frank was reduced to thirty-fourth on the all-time sales list.

Yet Frank was showman enough to welcome Elvis home from the Army in 1960 on Sinatra's TV show. For both entertainers, the teaming was a shrewd business move. Elvis was very much the viable name in spite of his absence during his Army service. Colonel Parker had stockpiled records, re-released his movies and kept Elvis from live performance for two years. The idea of Presley doing a spot on the TV show of the biggest singing star in the business was much to the Colonel's liking. His "boy" risked nothing. If the ratings zoomed, Elvis could take the credit; no change in ratings would mean that the show had drawn only the Sinatra crowd.

Elvis traveled by train from Memphis to Miami. The trip was likened to a presidential campaign. Fans lined the railway and Elvis stood on the rear platform waving to the crowd. Down in Miami, Frank's old-time pals, Dean Martin, Sammy Davis, Jr., Joey Bishop and Peter Lawford waited and wondered how this curious blend of talent would turn out.

The taping would be done in front of a Sinatra audience. No way would Frank permit Elvis' screaming fans to get inside the doors. Elvis would be locked into a tuxedo. Objecting to Frank's rules would cause a furor and Elvis could never risk appearing the heavy against a heavyweight.

The special was taped and both stars appeared at ease. Elvis sang two current hits, borrowed Sinatra's "Witchcraft" for the wind-up, and led the talented twosome into "Love Me Tender." Despite its low-key tone, the show, titled *Frank Sinatra's Welcome Home Party for Elvis*, was aired a few weeks later to ratings of 41.5, knocking out the competition.

Frank's show with Elvis was the last on his contract with the American Broadcasting System. Sinatra's contract with ABC began in 1970 when, to obtain Frank, the network made a fabulous deal—for him. It consisted of three-million dollars up front, the purchase of stock in his film producing company and carte blanche to produce the series himself. On paper, it read like a dream package—a deal that couldn't go wrong. Sinatra on the tube, swinging away in a weekly program which would showcase his superlative skills and those of his legion of friends.

The expectations were never fulfilled and the fault was laid at Sinatra's door. He refused to rehearse, using a stand-in to work for him in the sketches. *Variety*, after the first few airings, called it "something that can only be called intentional dullness." Critics and audiences alike complained how slipshod the programs were. The series was cancelled and by way of settlement, Sinatra appeared in a sequence of specials. The Elvis appearance was the last of these. ☆

Frank summoned Ella Fitzgerald for his 1967 television special. Their duets were memorable.

Sinatra refused to rehearse, using a stand-in to work for him in the sketches.

Frank clowns around with a supporting actor for a comedy sketch on his TV series.

While reviewers occasionally panned his films and columnists sometimes criticized his style, Frank won universal praise for his energetic charity work—much of it done anonymously. Here, at a benefit, he chats with Danny Thomas. Throughout the years, the two entertainers raised countless millions for charity.

THE POWER PLAY

Inspired by his mother's interest in politics, Sinatra longed to be close to those in power — but the questionable reputation of some of his associates caused him to be shunned by the men in high office.

In 1960, Frank welcomes Jacqueline Kennedy to the pre-inaugural gala which he produced in Washington.

Overnight, the President's enemies became Frank's.

Frank is presented to Queen Elizabeth at a Royal Command Performance in 1958.

Although Frank worked hard on USO tours during the World War II years, he felt a need to make a more positive contribution to America. So he tried politics.

It was a natural and perhaps inevitable step for the son of Dolly Sinatra, who had been active in New Jersey politics throughout her life. Frank was a Depression child and, like so many others, including Ava, he was a staunch supporter of Franklin D. Roosevelt, the President who in 1933 brought hope to a dispirited nation suffer-

His cronies began calling him "The Chairman of the Board." Even to his detractors, he's one of the most powerful and influential figures of the 20th Century.

When JFK was elected, Sinatra became one of the most favored knights at the Camelot Round Table.

In his years as a Democrat, Sinatra made no secret that he disliked Ronald Reagan. Once a Republican, he swerved full circle, attending Reagan's inauguration as California Governor in 1970. (L-R) Frank Sinatra, Gov. Reagan, singer Vikki Carr, Nancy Reagan, Dean Martin, John Wayne.

ing the anguish of a bitter era.

In September, 1944, Sinatra decided that FDR, who was running for a fourth term, could use some Sinatra support. Along with Rags Ragland, a comedian, and restaurateur Toots Schorr, he went to Washington and had no trouble gaining access to the White House and meeting the President, who reportedly asked him, "What's on the *Hit Parade* this week, Frank?"

Overnight, the President's enemies became Frank's. These enemies branded the visit as unseemly, a publicity stunt. But FDR, the man who counted, understood the value of show business supporters, and made it clear that he appreciated whatever help Sinatra and his friends could offer. Frank made a $7,500 non-deductible contribution to the campaign, joined the Independent Voters Committee, and on radio broadcasts campaigned for the President, calling himself "the little guy from Hoboken."

Frank became con-rned by the national ppetite for racial in-lerance and decided : might do something the way of a film. 'ith help from other ke-minded talents in ollywood, writer lbert Maltz and pro-ucer Charles Koerner, natra made a short m, *The House I Live* e, in which he played a ole and sang. It was a uiet jewel and eservedly won a pecial Academy ward.

lainly relishing his role as a public gure on the rostrum, rank appeared at a 'orld Youth Rally at Iadison Square -arden, visited the 'nited Nations as an bserver, and became hairman of the March f Dimes Youth Divi-on.

In 1948, a year in hich staunch Iollywood Democrats roclaimed themselves s Democrats for isenhower, Frank sup-orted Harry Truman. he betting odds gainst Truman were normous and Frank as one of the few who

cleaned up when Truman defeated Thomas Dewey.

Frank was active in the two Democratic campaigns of Adlai Stevenson, and had become such a reliable worker and organizer that he was inevitably welcomed by John F. Kennedy and the whole Kennedy family when he climbed aboard in the 1960 Presidential campaign.

He campaigned tirelessly for Kennedy and raised millions of dollars, some perhaps from questionable

Governor and Nancy Reagan and Vice President Spiro Agnew attended the dedication of Martin Sinatra Medical Center in 1971. Dolly Sinatra cut the ribbon at the event.

B rother-in-law Peter Lawford may have been JFK's nominal host, but it was Frank who put the President's schedule together.

Vice President Spiro Agnew in-spects Frank's Medallion of Valor awarded by Israel, 1972. After his resigna-tion under pressure, Agnew found a warm friend in Frank Sinatra and became a fre-quent house guest at Frank's Palm Springs estate.

sources. When JFK was elected, Sinatra became one of the most favored knights at the Camelot Round Table. He stag-ed the Inaugural Ball, a tremendous success, and afterward enjoyed ready access to the White House and to JFK whenever the President visited the West Coast. Brother-in-law Peter Lawford may have been JFK's nominal host, but it was Frank who put the President's schedule together. Sinatra install-ed a heliport at his Palm Springs estate, assum-ing JFK would one day visit there.

Instead, the Presi-dent became the guest of Bing Crosby — a Republican. Bobby Kennedy had decided that Frank's ties to the Mafia were embar-rassments his brother could not afford.

In the 1968 election, he became a Nixon man, although he had campaigned against him years earlier when Nixon ran for Califor-nia Governor. After Vice President Spiro Agnew was banished from office for taking bribes, he became a pal of Sinatra. Finally, Frank aligned himself with Ronald Reagan, once a target of snide lyrics interposed in his songs. Once again, Sinatra had access to

the White House, and there was no one around to threaten his position as an intimate. Nancy Reagan adored him.

I n 1981, Frank per-formed in a series of concerts held in Sun Ci-ty in Bophuthatswana, that little corner of South Africa, supposed-ly a Free State. He was paid two million dollars, and around the world cries of horror were heard. "Word needs to get out that Bophuthatswana is only a phony homeland," said tennis star Arthur Ashe. "Artists who ap-pear there are going to South Africa and are giving approval to a racist regime."

An American black leader sighed, "Where is that wonderful man who came to Alabama in the sixties to sing to us and to march?" To his critics, Frank shot back, "I sing to everybody, black and white, drunk or sober."

☆

MIA

Frank weathered charges of "cradle robbing," but it was Mia's desire to keep working that doomed the marriage.

In December, 1965, Frank turned fifty years old. As the date approached, there were plans to celebrate the milestone appropriately. Frank Sinatra had every reason to take time out in the fifth decade of his life and look back upon his extraordinary career. Besides family affairs and celebrations with his buddies, there would also be a CBS gala to celebrate the event.

1965 was also the year Frank met Mia Farrow, the twenty-year-old daughter of actress Maureen O'Sullivan and the late film director John Farrow. Mia was one of the seven Farrow children. "The first daughter," as she put it, "third from the top and fifth from the bottom." Not much was known about Mia beyond her connection to John and Maureen until she suddenly appeared on television as

Mia made known her preference for older men, citing Kirk Douglas and Yul Brynner as likely candidates for her affections.

After bouts of indecision, Frank finally decided to marry for a third time. Mia Farrow was thrilled and the ceremony took place on July 19, 1966. They honeymooned in London where Frank finished up a picture. He did his best to act the happy husband role, even posing for puppy picture with Mia, right. The white Pekingese was a gift from Liz Taylor.

the star of the first evening prime time soap opera, *Peyton Place*. In interviews, she made it clear that she was ambitious. "I want a big career, a big man and a big life. You have to think big—that's the only way to get it. I just couldn't stand being anonymous."

Mia had made known her preference for older men, citing Kirk Douglas and Yul Brynner as likely candidates for her affection if they were so inclined. *Peyton Place* was filming at Warners, when Frank Sinatra and his company checked in to film some pick-up shots for *Von Ryan's Express*. The presence of the big man on the lot excited the young cast of *Peyton Place*, who got in the habit of checking him out between takes. To catch Sinatra took effort and timing. He flew in from Palm Springs every day, did his shots on the run and quickly flew back. One day, Mia asked if she could fly back to the Springs with him. Sinatra knew who she was and had greeted her every day with a characteristic "Hi, kid." But until then, she was just another cute chick.

Frank gulped and asked himself, "Why not?" So Mia, the waif-like, skinny television star with milk-white skin, gorgeous long, blond hair and innocent blue eyes waltzed into Frank's life. She was like no other woman Frank had wooed and turned aside. Mia knew what she wanted—and that was Sinatra. With benefit of hindsight, it is clear that Frank, thirty years older than Mia, had normal doubts about the practicality of settling into a relationship with one so young. But Mia obviously knew how to overcome them. "She was manipulative," Angie Dickinson remarked.

As things grew more serious between the two, Sinatra admitted that he was lonely and didn't feel that the age difference was so important. To pals who objected, Sinatra reacted characteristically —swearing a

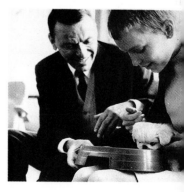

rank and Mia at the Frank
inatra Awards, 1967.

em and tuning them out of his
fe.

The Mia "business" complicated
family celebration of Frank's
irthday, which also marked the
wenty-fifth anniversary of his
ebut in big-time show business.
Hundreds of guests had been in-
ited to the affair, which was being
ut together by Nancy, Jr. and her
mother. Among the guests would
e President Johnson and Vice
resident Humphrey. The affair
vould also tie in with the CBS
ala.

When someone had the courage
o ask whether Mia should be in-
ited, Frank conceded that it was
ot a good idea. Everyone breath-
d a sigh of relief and everything,
ncluding the TV special, went ac-
ording to plan.

Frank, however, had stipulated
hat in a televised interview to ac-
ompany the gala, there could be
o personal questions, especially
bout Mia. But things didn't hap-
en quite as Sinatra expected.
There were questions and light-
earted kidding about "cradle robbing." Sinatra was furious, and
demanded to see the tape. CBS
efused. There were the usual
hreats of injunctions, etc., but the
ape, when aired, turned out to be
only a loving tribute. No mention
f Mia. Nothing about his fights.
Not a word about the Mafia. The
Los Angeles Times wrote: "Sinatra
nd his loyal clan could not have
ut together a more flattering look
t their leader."

arlier in the year, the Sinatra-
Mia affair was given a dramatic
iring in full view of the public,
when Frank chartered a yacht at
$2,000 a day to cruise off the shore
f New England. The cruise began
t Hyannesport, where Frank
could visit Kennedy patriarch,
ormer Ambassador Joseph Kennedy, who was unable to speak

MIA AFTER FRANK

When they divorced in 1968, Mia was 23 and
Frank 53. Shortly thereafter, Mia fell in love
with composer Andre Previn, married at the time to
his lyricist, Dore Previn. Dore expressed her heart-
break in songs, one of which told of a woman who
finds herself speeding—and screaming—in a "20
Mile Zone." In 1970, Mia and Andre wed. During
their nine-year-marriage, they had twins (Matthew
and Sascha, shown left with their parents) and
adopted several children, including a Vietnamese
orphan named Soon-Yi.

In 1982, Mia starred in Woody Allen's A Midsum-
mer Night's Sex Comedy. Thus began a personal
and professional relationship that would last a
decade. Although considered a couple, they did not
marry and maintained separate Manhattan resi-
dences. They did, however, adopt two children and
Mia gave birth to Woody's son.

Then Mia discovered that Soon-Yi, 19, was having an affair with Woody, 57. Although they were
roughly the same ages Frank and Mia had been
when they'd become involved, Mia was furious. Her
breakup with Woody became a sensation both in
the press and the courts.

When Woody challenged Mia's competence as a
mother, Frank contacted his ex-wife, offering support. Mia emerged from the battle, her career and
her brood intact.

It is certain that Frank, thirty years older than Mia, had normal doubts about the practicality of settling into a relationship with one so young.

Free from her contract, Mia was free to accept any offer—especially the opportunity to become Mrs. Frank Sinatra.

because of a stroke. Old friends of Frank, including Claudette Colbert and Rosalind Russell, were aboard. Mia called them "the *Late Show* gang."

Still, Mia had grown to like them, and the cruise promised to be joyous, despite the intrusions of reporters who sailed out to the yacht in small boats to film the action for the nightly news. The $64,000 question, of course, was now the question of marriage.

Tragedy befell the gala cruise when the yacht's third mate drowned while heroically saving the life of another crew member. The yacht steamed back to port, and Frank and his guests separated. Whatever plans Frank

Frank and Mia at the 1966 World Series, seated near the Dodgers dugout.

d Mia may have had for a wed-
ng were placed on hold.

Commented *Time* magazine: "It
d been the most closely observed
uise since Cleopatra floated
wn the Nile to meet Mark An-
ny."

In June, 1966. Frank and nine
ests were celebrating Dean
artin's birthday at the Polo
ounge in the Beverly Hills Hotel,
hen another guest, Frederick R.
eisman, protested the noise
om the Sinatra table and asked
em to tone it down.

A fight followed between the
o men that made headlines
ound the world. A house detec-
ve managed to break it up, but
ot before Sinatra had suffered a
ack eye and Weisman fell to the
oor unconscious.

The businessman, hospitalized,
ent into a coma after surgery and
mained unconscious for several
ays. It was a truly harrowing ex-
erience for Sinatra—much more
rious than his many previous
rawls, all widely documented in
e press.

Once Weisman was out of
anger—and it took some
me—and had recovered suffi-
ently to speak to the police, he

and his family decided not to press
charges. They were, it was said,
aware of Sinatra's reputation.

With this incident, as well as
the birthday bash behind
him, Frank could now give more
of his attention to Mia. He had
succeeded in extricating her from
Peyton Place, so she was free to accept any offer—especially the opportunity to become Mrs. Frank
Sinatra.

They were married in Las
Vegas on July 19, 1966, and the
story thereafter reads as though
the ceremony marked the end of
their romance. They honeymooned in London, while Frank starred
in *The Naked Runner* and were
guests of the Jack Warners in the
south of France.

When Frank discovered Mia
was serious about continuing her
career, the writing was on the wall.
He had not counted on an actress
wife. Over Frank's objections, she
starred in the TV production of
Johnny Belinda for producer David
Susskind, and later refused to walk
out on *Rosemary's Baby* when
Frank, resigned to her ambition,
wanted her to appear with him in
Detective Story.

Frank and Mia
were among the
celebrities lured to
Truman Capote's
masked ball in
1966.

Mia Farrow came
into her own as an
actress, playing in
the thriller
Rosemary's Baby.
Ralph Bellamy
played her doctor.

Rosalind Russell
became Mia's good
friend during the
Sinatra-Farrow
courtship, serving
as a sort of chap-
eron.

Mia had defied him. The inevitable happened. Frank wanted
a divorce. On the set of *Rosemary's
Baby*, Mickey Rudin, Sinatra's
lawyer, advised her that Frank was
starting divorce proceedings. Mia
cried, saddened that the great
romance of her young life was
over, and bewildered that Frank
lacked the courage to face her
himself.

The picture finished, Mia went
to Mexico, obtained a divorce, ac-
cepting nothing from Frank. She
reportedly tore up or gave away all
the gifts and other items that had
accumulated during their brief
marriage.

There were no more Mia jokes,
and the Sinatra kids could once
again say, "Mama Mia," without
raising eyebrows.   ☆

While Sinatra's incredible singing voice made him a star, his between-song badmouthing was nearly his undoing.

IN CONCERT

In June 13, 1971, Frank Sinatra gave a "farewell performance" on behalf of the Motion Picture Relief Fund at the Los Angeles Music Center in a magnificently crafted program. His career could be traced through the songs he sang, going back to the Dorsey days and across the years with "Nancy", "I'll Never Smile Again", "The Lady Is A Tramp" and "My Way". In the audience that night was his friend, Vice-President Spiro Agnew, along with then-governor of California, Ronald Reagan. So were Nancy, Sr. and Jr. and the other Sinatra offspring.

Frank was fifty-five and the announcement of his "retirement" a few months earlier had created

quite a stir. No one believed it for a moment, but Frank persisted in claiming he had been on the road for thirty-five years, made fifty-five films, over a hundred albums and a thousand singles. He wasn't ailing, Nancy, Jr. explained, simply tired.

There were other factors. His last three albums had not sold to the expected Sinatra figures, and his films had taken a drubbing from the critics, particularly *Dirty Dingus Magee*, a Western comedy which the reviewers labeled crude.

Two years later, Frank was back in the limelight, saying, "I didn't realize how much I'd miss the business—the records, the films, the saloons." He chose a television special, performed at

Madison Square Garden for his return. It wasn't a success, ratingswise or critically, but Frank, perhaps expecting it to turn out that way, was not disappointed. He announced that he'd next return to Las Vegas, a place he'd vowed never to enter after his last altercation there. This dispute had involved Caesar's Palace casino boss Sanford Waterman and resulted from a disagreement over Frank's credit line. Waterman pulled a gun on Sinatra, and the enraged singer walked out, threatening never to play Vegas again. But by 1973, Waterman and other Vegas enemies of Sinatra were no longer operating in the gambling capital, and that justified, in Frank's mind, the

Frankie vs Ol' Blue Eyes

Shortly before his death in 1974, jazz writer Ralph J. Gleason voiced bitter feelings about Sinatra in Rolling Stone *magazine.* "It is simply weird now to see him all glossed up like a wax dummy, with that rug on his head, looking silly; and the onstage movement, which used to be panther-tense, is now a self-conscious hoodlum hustle. What seemed like a youthful bravado twenty-five years ago seems like angry perversity now. Ol' Blue Eyes is a drag that Frankie never was."

And there were others who preferred Frankie to Blue Eyes. They resented his commentary between songs, the crudeness of his remarks directed at his enemies. He once joked that the press regarded him as the Eichmann of song. Folks who heard him sound off were inclined to agree.

A pretty, likeable woman who had long ago abandoned ambitions of a theatrical career, Barbara Marx was perfect for Frank.

urn. Whatever the press said out his voice, or his nasty obser-tions about newsmen, did not 'ect the success of his engage-ent. Frank was back on his own rain and could do no wrong.

Encouraged by the reception, ank next performed a ten-city ncert tour to benefit Variety ubs International. This was lowed by a tour of Europe. natra was back on the arts—the charts of the concert cuit. He appeared in large halls d stadiums—just like rock rs—and his shows sold out eks in advance. It had become exhilarating adventure, hough not everyone enjoyed the tervals when Frank stopped ging and started talking. The marks were usually diatribes ainst whoever he consider an emy at the time—Germans, ona Barret, the columnist, enedict Arnold, Barbara alters, Bruno Hauptman. Frank as not particular about whether a e was alive or dead.

Singing a medley of Sinatra andards, "I'll Hang My Tears ut To Dry" and "The Best Is Yet o Come," Sinatra stopped only r a sip of Jack Daniels and an "in ur face cigarette." To a disap-oving front-rower, he said, "You e your way, I'll die mine," then oved on to the finish of the edley "Luck Be a Lady" from uys and Dolls.

arbara Marx was in her forties when she met Frank Sinatra. t the time, she was the wife of eppo Marx, the fourth of the mous Marx Brothers. He had signed from their act in the mid 930's to become an agent. Later, e retired to Palm Springs and liv-l with Barbara in a house quite ose to Frank's estate.

Barbara, a sun-tanned blonde nd accomplished tennis player, as invited to Frank's place as a oubles partner for Spiro Agnew. he was in the throes of a divorce it ending her marriage to Zeppo ter thirteen years. They had met Las Vegas where she was a owgirl. Earlier, she had been a eauty contest winner. A pretty, keable woman who long ago had bandoned her ambitions for a eatrical career, she was ideally ited to Frank. Clearly, she alized this before Frank did.

After the divorce, she moved in ith Frank, much to the chagrin of olly Sinatra. Never adverse to oicing her opinions of Sinatra's oman friends, Dolly was ehemently opposed to his in-

Concerts have been the life blood of Sinatra's art.

Following a vicious dispute over his credit line, Frank vowed never to return to Vegas.

In 1989, Frank went on an all-star tour with Liza Minnelli and the late Sammy Davis, Jr.

volvement with the ex-Mrs. Marx.

But Frank paid little attention. They were married on October 10, 1976, in an elaborately arrang-ed ceremony, supposedly taking place at the home of the Kirk Douglases, but which actually took place in Walter Anneberg's estate at Rancho Mirage. It was Presidential-like in its ar-rangements, with uniformed, armed guards at the gates, and walkie-talkied security men all over the place.

Barbara threw herself into the role of Mrs. Frank Sinatra, and the couple's friends agreed that she performed that role extremely well. "She's exactly the kind of wife Frank has always wanted," ex-plained a friend. "A woman who knows her place and gets lost when she's not needed, or when Frank's nerves are strained."

A former housekeeper at the Sinatra estate reported on the *Current Affair* TV show that Barbara and Frank led fairly proscribed lives, meeting each evening for dinner. Frank slept most of the day and prowled around the estate at night, while Barbara preferred the daylight hours for her ac-tivities. The housekeeper noted that Frank maintained a specially air-controlled room for his couple of dozen toupees, and that a hair-dresser was in charge of keeping them on instant call.

Away from Palm Springs, Frank's activities during the Reagan years centered on visits to Washington and concert perfor-mances. In the late 80's, he ap-peared in concert with Liza Min-nelli and Sammy Davis, Jr. There had been an earlier tour involving Frank, Sammy and Dean Martin, but Dean quit mid-stream; illness

being the excuse offered. Actually, Dean quit because he felt he was at an age where he did not have to put up with Frank's barbs about his boozing.

The billing changed from Frankie to Ol' Blue Eyes, and often there was a conflict about which the audience preferred. Ol' Blue Eyes was a master showman; Frankie was someone who set the senses afire. But does it really mat-ter? Frankie or Ol' Blue Eyes, Sinatra was still the stuff of legends.

In his twilight years, Sinatra earned the right to look back upon all the events that made him a legend and to eliminate the "bad stuff"—the accusing headlines, the fist fights, the verbal attacks, and all the rest.

Take away the controversy and what are you left with? Simply the most popular singer of his time—and the most influential. An actor of considerable stature who, in fifty-five movies, achieved performances that some of his con-freres would die to have on their resumes. How much money did he earn for charity? No one could ever tally up that total. The con-certs were too numerous, and in too many places, both at home and abroad. And his private charities? The figures there must have run into the hundreds of thousands. Many unknowns have benefited from the Sinatra kindness. So too did Hollywood actors down on their luck, as well as plain, or-dinary panhandlers. Around the globe, Sinatra was hailed as the world's best tipper.

They say Frank was a lonely man, and that he had been so all his life. It may have been true, but his fans were always there for him—devoted, loyal and loving. ☆

UGLY REMARKS

At Caesar's Palace, audiences got a glimpse of the unretired Frank Sinatra's unretired temper. Rona Barrett had just published her autobiography, and in it, she maintained that the kidnapping of Frank Sinatra, Jr. had been a hoax. Sinatra took time out of his show to tell the audience that Rona was "so ugly that her mother had to tie a pork chop around her neck to get the dog to play with her. Congress should give her husband a medal just for waking up and looking at her." Barbara Walters was another person on Frank's hate list. He called her the "ugliest woman on television." In Vegas, the offensiveness of these remarks was tolerated, but elsewhere, audiences were embarrassed when Ol' Blue Eyes began one of his diatribes.

THE FAMILY MAN

Frank's family has survived decades of adversity, and emerged a tight-knit group, loyal to the Chairman of the Board.

In a sense, Frank had always been an absentee husband and father. And so, while the break-up of Sinatra's marriage to Ava Gardner was emotionally shattering, it did not materially affect the family's lifestyle. In spite of it — and perhaps because of it — they remained a strong family unit.

Nancy Sinatra can take credit for raising her children well and bringing them to young adulthood with her own sense of values firmly implanted. Not that there weren't problems. There were many, and in all the forms known to families, both on their economic level and below it. But the family bond was identified as the important element in their lives, and it has been respected.

Nancy and the children adored Frank. They were proud of him, loyal when his mercurial disposition made headlines, and devoted when he needed them most. Frank, in turn, sought to be a responsible parent. He was lavish with his gift-giving, often

This was a special night in Vegas annals — the evening in 1970 when the entire Sinatra clan gathered at Caesar's Palace to celebrate Nancy's opening in the main showroom. In usual order are Dad, Nancy, Nancy, Sr., Tina and Frank, Jr. Dad, they said, was suffering a tendon ailment.

Frank Sinatra and daughters, Tina and Nancy, break ground in 1970 for the Martin Anthony Sinatra Medical Center, built to honor the entertainer's late father.

Nancy Sinatra can take credit for raising her children well and bringing them to young adulthood with her values firmly implanted.

After Frank and Barbara Marx announced wedding plans in 1976, elaborate steps were taken to keep the time and place a deep, dark secret. Said Frank, "It's nobody's business."

The Sinatra, Jr. Kidnapping—
IT WAS NOT FAKE

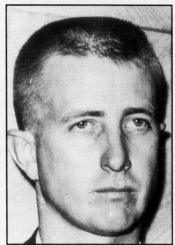

Barry W. Keenan, having served time for kidnapping Frank Jr. is now out of prison, in business and remorseful.

When 19-year-old Frank Sinatra, Jr. was reported kidnapped on December 8, 1963, reaction suggested that the young offspring of Frank Sinatra, just beginning his own singing career, had engineered the caper as a publicity stunt. Nothing could have been further from the truth, as subsequent events have proved.

Frank, Jr. and a trumpet player, John Foss, responded to a knock at the door at Harrah's Lodge in Lake Tahoe, where Frank was performing. They admitted a man with a .38 revolver who hurled Frank out of the room into a waiting car, which sped off into the night. Thus began fifty-three hours of terror for Frank, Jr., his father and his family. The kidnapper, Barry Worthington Keenan, a 23-year-old drifter, had coerced two other men to join him in the crime. Foss, who had been tied up, freed himself within minutes and was soon on the phone to the police. Long before the criminals contacted Sinatra, Sr. for $240,000 in ransom money, the kidnapping was known. So was Keenan's identity, discovered in fingerprints left at the hotel.

The ransom was paid. Young Sinatra was released after being held in a house in Canoga Park, California, and the perpetrators captured by the FBI, brought to trial and imprisoned.

Recently, Keenan appeared on the Current Affairs TV program to recall the crime, his part in it and, hopefully, to make amends. He explained that as a recovering alcoholic, setting the record straight was an obligation.

In the interview, Keenan explained how quickly the plot blew up in his face, but that the ransom money was in his possession for a time. He took it to a safe house, where he "played" with the large collection of bills, "whirling the money around and walking over it." He explained that he needed the large sum of money to pay off his own debts and those of his family.

Finally, he admitted that it had been a stupid thing to do, and the years in prison afforded him ample opportunity to consider his folly. He regretted the onus that fell on Frank, Jr. The end result of his inside account of the kidnapping was to finally dispel any lingering doubts, if they still existed, that young Frank had any part in the bizarre scheme.

Keenan is now a successful businessman.

---

trageously so. As the song says, Frank did it "his way." Everyone in the family knew that being a Sinatra was something very special, and because of it, they would all lead very special lives.

Nancy Sinatra remained very much the woman she was determined to be when she divorced Frank. She became a distinguished Hollywood matron, devoting herself wholly to her children in their formative years, and later becoming active in charity and community affairs.

Nancy, Jr. became her father's right hand in his financial and creative empire. Frank, Jr. was his father's musical director, and Tina, the youngest, became the Sinatra archivist.

Frank, mindful of his own lack of formal schooling, had hoped for college educations for his children. But none professed interest, though Nancy, Jr. and Frank, Jr. both tried their hands at it. Obviously, as Frank's fortunes grew,

the children would have to become a part of them, so their on-the-spot training probably served them as well as any higher education might have. The extraordinary security of huge lifetime trust funds has not made them dullards, but neither has it necessarily opened the door to personal happiness.

Nancy, Frank's favorite, survived an early unsuccessful marriage to Tommy Sands, a singing idol of the bobby soxers. She was twenty when Frank proudly gave her away at a ceremony in Las Vegas. Tommy wore his Air Force uniform, being in the service at the time.

The father figure of Frank hovered ever-present over the marriage. Frank helped Tommy get film jobs, and Nancy turned to Frank constantly for advice. She could not be persuaded to move away from her father's influence, and after five years, Sands simply moved out. There were tears and recriminations.

The father figure of Frank hovered everpresent over the marriage. Frank helped Tommy get film jobs, and Nancy turned to Frank constantly for advice.

"These Boots Are Made For Walkin'," sang Nancy on her big hit record.

Nancy Sinatra, Jr. and Tommy Sands cut their wedding cake after the 1960 ceremony. Nancy, Sr. is the beaming mama at the event.

Nancy, Jr. and second husband, Hug Lambert, outside the church in Cathedral City where they were married 1970.

In 1970, Nancy married Hu Lampert, a produce choreographer. A daughte Angela Jennifer, was born 1973, and the following ye another daughter. Frank was proud grandfather.

Frank, Jr. appears to have be a victim of the blatant favoritis shown to Nancy when they we growing up, yet when it came tir to make a career for himse Frank gave him steady suppo Young Frank, like Nancy, hop to become a singer. It was fai easy for them to obta engagements, accompanied by t hoopla and publicity the Sinat name created. Nancy even a peared on a show with her fath and their record, *Somethin' Stupid* 1967 was Frank's first gold sing Neither offspring possessed eith the magnetism or the vocal skills their father. They peaked at t beginning, and there was no pla to go but down.

Frank was horrified wh Frank, Jr. was cited in a patern suit. Twice more the famous s would be hauled into court similar charges. Frank insisted th Junior accept responsibility a contribute to the children's support.

Tina has been appointed "Keeper of the Flame" and charged with the task of safeguarding the Sinatra legend. According to Kitty Kelly, Sinatra was eager for his life story to be told during his lifetime. A biography was ruled out because of his distrust of writers. Tina, then, was preoccupied for several years working on a mini-series based on Frank's life as an entertainer, philanthropist and intimate of presidents. From time to time, one heard of its coming to life, but even now it appears to be still only in the planning stages.

Like Nancy, Tina has been unsuccessful in marriage. Her one trip to the altar, with Wes Farrell, ended in divorce after only eleven months. A later engagement to Robert Wagner was called off when he began dating his ex-wife, Natalie Wood.

Frank's devotion to his parents was well chronicled. He was severely affected by his father's death in 1969. Frank had flown Marty Sinatra to a Houston hospital, hoping special facilities there would help his father's ailing

Tina Sinatra often dated Robert Wagner, but their engagement was broken off. Wagner re-married former wife Natalie Wood in 1972.

Frank was horrified when Frank, Jr. was cited in a paternity suit. Twice more the famous son would be hauled into court on similar charges.

Frank Sinatra, Nancy, Jr. and Frank, Jr. (below).

heart. It was too late. The former fire captain did not survive.

But Frank was not prepared for the death of his mother, Dolly, the grand matriarch of the family, in January, 1977. Over the years, Dolly had resisted Frank's suggestions that she move to California. Dolly preferred New Jersey, as her friends were all there. But after Marty's death, she agreed to the move.

Dolly loved Las Vegas and reveled in her son's appearances there. It was on her way to one of these that the Lear jet she was aboard crashed into a mountainside. Frank took the loss hard, saying over and over again, "It wasn't as though she flew all the time. This was a lady who flew maybe a half dozen times in her life."

Dolly's death stirred something in Frank's conscience that led him to return to the Catholic church.

He began attending Mass, but as a divorced man, he could not receive Communion. This obstacle was removed when Frank received a Papal annulment of his marriage to Nancy. Of course, he had hoped to keep it a secret and, of course, it became another Sinatra news shocker. The action by the Vatican horrified Nancy, the children, and thousands of Catholics in similar positions who lacked Frank Sinatra's wealth and influence.

As she always has, Nancy Sinatra held her head high as the annulment was discussed. Riding out the tides of Frank's mercurial career, his private life, his demons and his grief, has become a way of life for her. On her shoulders rests the responsibility for keeping the Sinatra family intact—a strong unit, forever loyal to the Chairman of the Board. ☆

Frank in 1987.

Frank and Barbara Sinatra in 1980. Although Frank's career kept him on the road weeks at a time, Barbara made their time together special.